An Encouraging Prophetic Word To the Church of America

Art Miner

Matthew Robert Payne

This book is copyrighted by Matthew Robert Payne. Copyright © 2019 All rights reserved.

Any part of this book can be photocopied, stored, or shared with anyone for the purposes of encouraging people. You are free to quote this book, use whole chapters of this book on blog posts, or use this book to spread the message of Jesus with this world. No consent from the author is required of you.

Please visit http://personal-prophecy-today.com to sow into Matthew's writing ministry, to request a personal prophecy or life coaching, or to contact him.

Cover designed by akira007 at fiverr.com.

Edited by Lisa Thompson at www.writebylisa.com. You can email Lisa at writebylisa@gmail.com for your editing needs.

All scripture is taken from the New King James Version. Copyright © 1982 by Thomas Nelson, Inc. Used by permission. All rights reserved.

The opinions expressed by the author are not necessarily those of Christian Book Publishing USA.

Published by Christian Book Publishing USA. Christian Book Publishing USA is committed to excellence in the publishing industry. Book design Copyright © 2019 by Christian Book Publishing USA. All rights reserved.

Paperback ISBN: 13: 978-1-925845-14-3

Dedication

I dedicate this to the people of my prophetic group that I run on Zoom. You are special to me. I want to thank Art for this book.

Table of Contents

Dedication

Table of Contents

Introduction

A Prophetic Word to the Church of America

Closing Words

I'd Love to Hear from You

How to Sponsor a Book Project

Suggested Further Reading

Acknowledgments

About Matthew Robert Payne

BLURB

Introduction

I want to welcome the people who are reading this book. This short book has a prophetic word given by a friend of mine, Art Miner, who is a prophet. I have known him for a few months, and he has been active in a prophetic training group that I have been running online. In the time that I have known him, I have seen him give many accurate prophetic words to people that I know.

He's been used for many years to give personal prophetic words to people. In my experiences with him, I have found him to be very accurate and very encouraging. Part of the prophetic journey is to not only release personal prophetic words but to release corporate prophetic words. Today I've asked him to speak on behalf of God as a vessel and a mouthpiece to give an encouraging message to the church of America.

This prophecy was originally a video that was uploaded to YouTube and has now been typed out as a message that became this book. As I went through this prophetic word, I edited small parts of it to make it more readable. I also added more from my perspective to make it more effective in communicating what I feel the Spirit of the Lord wants to say.

You might feel that this is not a "thus saith the Lord" type of prophecy, and I will agree with you in part. But this is a message from the Lord through two of his prophets. It is vital and relevant, and I compel the people of God who want to see change to read it.

Matthew Robert Payne
March 2019

A Prophetic Word to the Church of America

Art:

I would like to start out by saying that for many years, Jesus has been speaking to me about when he was ready to go to the cross to be crucified. He went to his disciples and said, "Will you not watch and pray with me but one hour?" (Matthew 26:40, author's paraphrase). Yet they all went to sleep and didn't seem concerned. I feel that's what's wrong with the church today. Basically the church has gone to sleep, and God is saying, "Wake up. Wake up, my people. There's much I have for you to do."

We have become all caught up in the job we are doing in the church, and we have been lulled to sleep. This message isn't just to the Baptists, the Methodists, the Lutherans, or the Catholics. This is to his body, and he's saying, "Wake up," because so many things are going on here in America.

In January 2019, New York passed a law permitting the killing of a nine-month-old fetus. People might call that late-term abortion. I call it murder. God is extremely upset and is weeping right now. He's weeping for his church because the church is being silent, and they've been silent for a long time. We know that the Bible says that when a good man does nothing when he should act, it's sin.

We have become complacent, saying, "Oh, I can't speak up. My voice won't be heard. I can't do this. I can't change that. Who will listen to me?"

But you know, the Bible says that if one can set a thousand to flight, two can set ten thousand to flight (Deuteronomy 32:30, author's paraphrase). We need to wake up; we need to hear the voice of God. The Word of God says he knows his sheep, and his sheep know his voice. (See John 10:14–16.) A lot of people know how to cry out to God. They know how to say, "God, I need this. God, I need that. Do this. Do this or that in my life."

But as a man or a woman of God, if you call yourself a Christian, that term means to be Christ-like. So wherever you go, you should influence those around you. In other words, you need to cast a shadow. We need to cast the shadow of the cross. Our own shadow needs to die. We need to put on the shadow of the cross, which is Jesus Christ. We become so complacent, and maybe we are worried about what we're going through or what we think God ought to do for us. But instead of asking for things to make us happy, we need to be on the firing line.

I see God putting an army together, and you can choose to be in this army or not. I believe Christ is calling out to churches. Lindell Cooley wrote a song called "Will You Ride?" that talks about a church that will ride with him, that will mount their horse and will let the commander-in-chief lead them. Jesus is coming back for a victorious church.

We need to pray. I don't want to talk about politics a lot, because I'll be honest with you: I'm not a Democrat, and I'm not a Republican. I vote for the person, and right now, we need to pray for and undergird our president, Donald Trump. When these kinds of abortion laws are being passed in New York in a country that is supposed to be a Christian country, something is drastically wrong. The United States is supposed to be a leader of the world. We are supposed to be the great city on a hill that Christ spoke of in Matthew 5:14–16. But here we are, saying that this is okay. You might say, "Well, I didn't vote for abortion. I didn't vote for this." But if you are quiet and say nothing, you are going along with the crowd.

You know who changes things? The people that speak up, the people who are willing to do something, the people that are willing to give of themselves. If this country does not turn from its wicked ways, it's getting ready for a fall. The United States used to be a great leader, a great nation among nations. We still are, but what is happening in the United States today is vomit in God's mouth.

What kind of influence do you have? What kind of shadow do you portray? When you walk into a room, can people tell you're a Christian even if you don't open your mouth? Does your family know? Does your family—your grandpas and dads and aunts and kids and grandkids—know what kind of man you are? Women, do they know that their meme or nana or grandma is a woman of God? Do they see God in you?

Let me say this about family and knowing God. I have seven grandchildren, and I had a bad headache today. My two-and-a-half-year-old granddaughter laid her hands upon my forehead and prayed for me. She said, "Dear, Jesus. Let Papa's headache go away, and do it quick." That miracle came through a two-and-a-half-year-old girl. Now we should all be walking in the faith of that child as a country of believers.

I heard a message about a guy who walked into church. He had on old cowboy boots, some torn-up jeans, a cowboy shirt, and a big cowboy hat. He sat down in the third row. In this church, the people thought, *Oh, my God, what's this guy doing here? Doesn't he know you're supposed to try to put on your best for God?*

After the service, the pastor came to him and said, "My people think that you need to really consider what you wear when you come to this church."

He said, "Oh, okay, okay."

So the next Sunday, he came dressed the exact same way, and the preacher said, "Hey, I thought I told you to talk with God about what to wear."

He replied, "Well, sure, I did talk to God, and he told me that he really doesn't know what your dress code is for this church because he hasn't been here. He wasn't invited."

That is a sobering story, but I want to share with you that our lives are sometimes that way. We can have as much of God in our lives as we want, but why don't we choose to have him dominate our lives?

I'm not a good-looking guy by earthly standards, but I know one thing: God does not look on the outward appearance. He looks on the inward appearance. God is looking at his inward body, the body of Christ. I'm talking about Christians now. He's saying, "What is the matter with you? Wake up."

It's a bit like this. Has anyone gotten in their bed to go to sleep and covered up their head? I think that's what churches do. They're covering up their heads. They're covering up the lordship of Christ in their lives.

We have to be very concerned about what's going on. I am aware that if you are reading this, you might come from any kind of religious background. It's not what religion you are from because religion doesn't save you; it doesn't do anything for you. It really doesn't even feed you. Religion is man-made for a certain church. Churches have all kinds of names and denominations: The First Church of the Holiness, the Baptists, the Pentecostals, the Methodists, the Lutherans, the Catholics, whatever church it might be. God is saying, "I don't care about your name. I don't care about your name. You can write anything above a door, but that does not make your gathering place my house."

For instance, if you write, "This place is a bakery," and you have no baked goods, it's not a bakery. It's just a name above the door. God wants to instill himself into people, and he's saying to the church of America, "Stand up and be a voice."

People might have all kinds of handicaps or things wrong with them, but they're still used by God. I had a little niece born with part of her brain outside her head, the part that had to do with speech. They had to cut that hunk of the brain off because they said she wouldn't live. After the surgery, they said she wouldn't live for three hours. She lived to be fifteen years old, and her name was Angel. Every person turned up for her funeral when she died in Rockford, Illinois. The newspaper headline read, "Rockford Lost an Angel Today."

Every police officer, every teacher, every neighbor, every family member, came out for her. It was one of the biggest funerals that Rockford, Illinois, ever had. And Angel couldn't talk, but she was a light. She was a light to everyone she met. All she did was show love. That's exactly the life that God wants us to have. That is the effect our lives should have on people and on communities.

You don't have to always look pretty or wear a three-piece suit. You don't have to have a lot of money. You don't have to have possessions to be special, but you have to know who you are and where you are, and you simply need to hear what God is speaking to you.

I come from a family of nine kids. Growing up, my dad wanted us to be a family together. Every night, he wanted his family at the dinner table. The Word of God says he prepares a table before us (Psalm 23:5). How many of us are really sitting at the table of God? How many hear the Father?

My dad would bless our meals and read the Word, and then we would eat. Back then, I thought, "Oh, Dad, come on. Just get this over with. I'm hungry; I want to eat." Yet sadly, that's the way the church is. Do they really want to hear what God's saying? Do they really want to walk the way God wants them to walk?

People are always saying, "God, use me, use me, use me." Here in the United States, people don't write their government—their representatives and senators—and say, "Hey, this sickens me. This sickens me." You might say, "I don't know how to write. I don't know what to say." I challenge you to just start writing to your elected representatives and let them know what you don't approve of.

People have things on their heart that God wants written down and shared on Facebook or on a blog. I don't care how you look or how you think you need to look, God can use you as a vessel. All you have to do is be willing to be filled with his Word and share it with others. You don't need to be a prophet to bring a message or correction. You have a heart. You have a relationship with God. You know how to hear him. You know how to communicate on Facebook. It's time that God spoke through you instead of you just giving your opinion and sharing your comings and goings on there.

You don't need to worry what people will think about you because I tell you, if you live your life worrying about what people think about you, you will live and die miserable.

Before they do anything worthwhile, some people say, "Oh, I need to find a church." Yes, I agree that it's important to find a place to worship, but the greatest thing you can do is have intimacy with your Father. Be intimate with the Father and Jesus. Talk to them.

I had a good earthly dad. Some people aren't blessed that way. Some people grew up with all hell breaking loose around them. But people, do you know what? When you gave your heart to Jesus Christ, you became a new creature, and you now have a heavenly Father. You have a daddy. Your Father doesn't judge your appearance. You don't have to be like anyone else because God created every one of us as individuals. Of the billions of people in this world, no two people are exactly alike. That should tell you something.

We're all individuals. You need to choose this day who you serve. As for me and my house, I'll serve the Lord. I want to tell my wife and the women listening something. I've been married for forty-seven years, and my wife can tell you that at times, she wishes I'd just go down the road. But I know one thing, the greatest thing you can do for your husband is to honor him. Don't speak any bad words about him.

I have a message for the dads also. The greatest thing you can do is to love your kids' mama. Love her.

Tragically, here in the United States, you can easily get a divorce. They ought to charge a lot of money to get married. That way, when people got married, they'd take marriage more seriously. People are too used to becoming upset and leaving without even trying to resolve their problems and work through them. This needs to change.

People will say, "Well, I went to this church, and the pastor spoke this, and it really hurt me." The pastor will say something hurtful, and instead of approaching the pastor and addressing it, they will take their family and leave the church. This should not be happening in our lives.

You know what? Sometimes we need to grow up because discipline is good for the soul. Discipline is good. If someone can't be disciplined or can't hear what God is saying to them, something's wrong, drastically wrong.

And we've all been hurt. I'd like to talk about that. We've all been hurt, but Jesus can take a broken vessel and put it on the potter's wheel. He can put his hand to that vessel, and that vessel will be as if it had never been broken. Here in the United States, we have all kinds of gadgets to fix things. We have all kinds of ways to fix our mistakes. But Jesus is the only one who can take a broken vessel, and just by putting his hand to it, he can make it as if it's never been broken. We need to fix things the right way and not with our clever ways. We have to resolve our marriage conflicts the right way and not walk out and divorce. We have to solve an unwanted pregnancy the right way with counseling or adoption and not through abortion. We need to talk through issues with our leaders in church and resolve the problems and not just walk out and leave. Each of us, as individuals, should be led by, counseled by, and directed by the Holy Spirit.

Every one of us has been broken in one way or another. We might have been abused, and we don't want to talk about it. We might have gone through a bad marriage, and we try to blame it on someone other than ourselves. We might think, "God, why don't I have a mate? What's going on? Aren't I worth it to anyone?"

But God says, "Hey, I'm the potter, and you're my vessel." I don't know what this is about, but God is telling me to tell the church, "We need to set our pots out; we need to fill our vessels." The vessels today are half full. What good is a half-full vessel? I'd rather have my vessel flowing over, spilling out.

This is to someone reading this book right now. Set your vessel out. Let God fill it. Don't let it be half full as the unwise virgins did. You don't even have enough for yourself. You need to have enough energy and love from the Holy Spirit to fill your own life and sustain yourself. You need to be filled up to the brim so that you are spilling over into the lives of other people. You should not be living a life full of struggles and drowning; you should be full of joy even in the midst of trials if you have them. You need to be the light of Christ everywhere you go. You need to be the answer for other people, not just coping with life and living selfishly. For more on living this way, you should read these two books by Matthew Robert Payne: *13 Tips to Becoming the Light of Christ* and *Influencing Your World for Christ*.

Now I'm going to speak to the pastors. If you don't have a heart and a love for God's people, get out from behind the pulpit. You don't belong there. If it's just a job, if it's a financial source to you, get out of that job or that source of income and stop being a rebellious son. You might have built the biggest church or pastored lots of people or led so many to the Lord, and now you have lost your zeal and your purpose. You need to find refreshment in the Lord through some time out. Refocus and get filled with the love for your flock. Otherwise, resign and leave that position.

This is for the people in the pews who don't think that they are in any worthwhile ministry. God says if you give one cup of water in his name, you have done something great that will be rewarded in heaven. (See Matthew 10:42.) How many of you have given cups of water or bottles of soda away, to use today's language? You don't have to give away thousands of dollars. Just set a cup of water in front of someone that needs a drink and say, "Do you know how much God loves you?" This is a really great way to minister to the poor and homeless in your city. Just buy them a Coke and minister love to them.

Until you can learn to show your emotions and be open and vulnerable, you're not really being loving. When you love, you will be hurt sometimes. You might not like what that homeless person says or how they receive you. It's not about that. It's more about how many people you can minister God's love to.

I was in a doctor's office the other day for physical therapy because I was in a car wreck. As I sat waiting, in walked this young man with holes in the knees of his pants. His hair was red, purple, and green, and he had tattoos all over him. When I first looked at him, I thought, *Wow*.

But you know, instantly God said, "How do you know I don't love him? How do you know how I feel about him, Art?"

As I waited there, I was humbled to see that young man witness to somebody, and I thought again, *Wow*.

We look at people, and we are so quick to judge. Oh, this girl wears her skirts too short, or she acts loose or whatever judgment we make. How do you know what God thinks of her? How do you know? Judgment needs to begin in the house of the Lord. We do not have the right to judge one another. Jesus commanded us to love one another. That's why we were put on this earth. God wanted someone to love. God saw that Adam needed someone to love, so he made a woman.

The bottom line is you can know the Bible from front to back. You can pray up a storm; you can even lay hands on people so that they are healed. But if you don't have love—true, genuine love—you have nothing. (See 1 Corinthians 13.)

That is what's wrong with the churches today. We have forgotten how to love one another even with just a cup of water. We need to look at our lives. How deeply are we in love with Jesus Christ? How much of the love of Christ is flowing through us? How much of our lives does Jesus possess? How full of oil are we? How much can we give away? Are we so empty that we cannot even cope with our own lives, let alone the lives of others? Something has to change. Something has to change with you today. It is time for you to take an honest inventory and change how you are living.

You need to learn how to have intimacy with Jesus. You need to draw so close to Jesus so that his thoughts are flowing through your mind and so that your heart is filled with his emotions. You need to be so close to Jesus that when you are speaking and interacting with people, you will begin to treat them as Jesus would treat them. It's not good enough just to go to church; you need to bring the love of Jesus into the world. You need to be so close to Jesus that you overflow with his love and compassion.

Another great quality you can have is empathy. When you can empathize with a person because of your own previous struggles and pain, you can really encourage him or her.

Conversely, I've had people come up to me and say, "Oh, I know what you're going through, brother Art. I know. Blah, blah, blah." Sometimes they should just say hi and then walk on by and not bother with the garbage that they say when they don't know what I am going through.

I was in a church once, and my pastor said this to me. "Art, I want to use you this morning. When people ask you how you feel, tell them you feel like you want to kill yourself."

So people walked by and said, "Oh, brother Art, how are you today?"

And I said, "Oh, I feel like I want to just kill myself."

"Oh, praise God," they answered. "That's wonderful." They didn't even pay attention to what I had said.

Many times, we say we hear the voice of God. How do you know you have heard his voice? How do you know? A lot of people just say hi like the people did in my church when the pastor said to test people.

Many people in churches all around this country are not even listening to each other. They are not showing any sort of love. It might surprise you, but some people come to church so that they can feel and experience some love, and we are passing them by and not even listening to their cries for love and help.

Do you really love as God wants you to love? Do you really hear his voice? Do you know what? The older I get, the more I want that intimacy with God. Church, you have to have intimacy with God. You have to. You have to show love to God and others.

Matthew Robert Payne wrote a book called *7 Keys to Intimacy with Jesus*. You should buy it, read it, and apply the truths in it until you have intimacy with Jesus.

When we take communion, it should be important. To me, communion is very sacred; I take it more often than just during scheduled times at church. I take it in my own home, sometimes with just me and my wife. During communion, we say, "Here's my body, broken for you, take and eat this token in remembrance of me" (1 Corinthians 11:24, author's paraphrase). Who are we remembering? We weren't broken; we didn't go to that cross. I could never do that. I couldn't save anyone by being crucified. But Jesus Christ paid an ultimate price for our love, and yet—yet we make light of what he did.

It's time for the church, the nations, that say they're godly to step forth and love as God wants them to love. It is time for intimacy with your Father and to become transformed through that intimacy into the image of Jesus Christ.

My dad passed away when I was thirty-five years old. My dad never told me he loved me until the day that he died. On that day, he called me into his room, and he said, "Son, I just want you to know I'm proud of you, and I love you." Those were the most wonderful words I had ever heard. All my life, the only thing I wanted my earthly father to do was to acknowledge that he was proud of me and that he loved me. When he said that, it changed me!

I personally love and encourage people and go about sharing the Word of the Lord with them. Yet as much as I share love with people, I want to be loved by them as well.

People might be reading this book today and saying, "God, I'm going through this. I feel as if you don't love me." But do you know what? He paid the price. I would just say to you today that you need to develop intimacy with God and be a man or a woman of your word. It's not about what church you go to, what clothes you wear, giving the prettiest speech, or whether your hair is out of place. It's about whether you truly show love to one another. That's what will save this world, and you can do it one person at a time.

One guy met me and saw that I had a reasonable amount of authority and anointing on my life. He asked me, "What church do you attend?"

I am not sure if he was bragging, but he said, "Well, I pastor four thousand people."

I said, "Well, praise God. I think that's pretty neat." And I did, I meant what I said; it was neat.

He asked, "Where do you pastor? What's your church?"

And I thought for a minute and said, "I pastor billions of people."

And he said, "What? Who are you?" He was stunned and trying to figure out who I was, this person who claimed to pastor billions.

I said, "Jesus Christ is my dad." And I continued, "Every place I walk and every place I go and every time I open up my mouth, I want people to know that I have a daddy. I have an Abba Father."

There you have it, dear reader. That's how I try to minister. I don't want to count the people that I have led to Jesus. Numbers are not important to me. Helping people find their own relationship with Jesus makes me so happy. Just giving people a loving message from him wherever I am and wherever I go keeps me going and happy with life. You can learn how to do this in Matthew Robert Payne's book, *Prophetic Evangelism Made Simple*.

A church will have a revival meeting, and sometimes five hundred people give their life to Jesus. But what do they do with those people? How much time did they give them after that? So many sheep come to the Lord and give their life to him, and then they're looking for love. They find that there is no love in the church. The church needs to learn how to love people. The church members need to learn how to love people like Jesus did. When a person says hi at church, you should listen to that person and have a real conversation with them like you would with one of your closest friends.

The church needs to wake up, be intimate with God, and love one another. Matthew Robert Payne is writing a book that addresses how the church lacks love. The book is called *Why Revival Tarries: A Prophetic Message for Today*. (Matthew's note: This book was released on February 19, 2019.)

Matthew: You really blessed us today, Art. And I look forward to hearing more.

Art mentioned my most recent book above. The theme of the book, *Why Revival Tarries: A Prophetic Message for Today*, is that we need to obey Jesus and that we need to learn to love. If we had stadium revivals now with millions of people coming to the Lord, the fact is that they'd leave after coming to church for three weeks. They would say as they walked out the door, "Those are a bunch of hypocrites."

They would know that the church talks about Jesus, but in the three weeks that they stayed, they would say they had never met him at that church, and they'd leave. Jesus refuses to bring home the people on the highways and the byways just so they will be hurt once more.

Art: Yes.

Matthew: Jesus wants to protect all the hurting people: those brokenhearted prostitutes, homosexuals, drug addicts, the sex-trafficked people, and broken and abused children all over the world. He says, "I need my people to learn how to love because when I bring these people home, they will be messy. They will be crying. They will have demons, and they'll be possessed. They will need a lot of love and a lot of understanding. And church, you are just not ready for these people yet. You need to learn how to love."

So we need more than a revival; we need the whole church to be trained and equipped to love like Jesus.

Art: Amen.

Matthew: We won't see world revival until the church has become a place that can be a nursery to the children and a sustaining, loving family to the brokenhearted. If they don't accept me, Art, if they don't accept you, they won't accept others, man. I've only stayed alive for the last twenty years although I've wanted to commit suicide nearly every day of that time. I've only stayed alive for the sexually molested and brokenhearted people. Jesus says that my people can't come home yet because the church will not accept them. They don't look for people that Jesus wants to bring home. These outcasts—who are really Jesus's people—don't speak, act, talk, or dress the right way. They don't have enough money to put in the tithing plates. They're addicted and in trouble.

People walk past them every day. They're the homeless people, those you look down on. They're all the broken people in the pubs, the clubs, the strip joints, the brothels. They're the pedophiles that are sexually trafficking children. They're sexually trafficked children. They're the mothers who are having abortions. They're the children who are rejected. They're the single moms and families all across America without fathers. They're all the sons being brought up in houses without fathers. They're the children being brought up by lesbian couples or homosexual couples. They're the homosexual couples, the homosexual females and males that are drug-addicted. They're the people in prison, those who are sick and mentally ill. There are millions of—a billion—brokenhearted people that need to come home.

And Jesus loves them too much, and he won't bring them home until the church will love them too.

Art: You know, Matthew, God has showed me something that I know is on your heart too. If we cannot show these people love, we might as well close the doors to every church out there. It's not just about loving the people who go to church. It's easy to love someone who loves in return.

Wake up, church! How many would go up to a smelly homeless person who hasn't bathed in weeks or even months and put their arms around that person and say, "Do you know how much God loves you? Do you know? I'm here to tell you. I want to show you."

That's what's wrong with the church today. They want to love their chosen; they want to love the ones who are there. But what are they doing about the ones who really need the love of Jesus? I don't believe Jesus would go into half the churches today. That's because their love has grown cold. We need to love the unlovable.

Matthew: Yeah. I'm really touched. This is not only going to be a video, Art. It is good enough for me to produce an e-book and a short paperback. I want to take the time to have it typed up and at least produce it as an e-book, a prophetic wake-up call to the church of America.

Art: Yes. That would be great.

Closing Words

Matthew:

This was just a short message for you. I hope that it has woken you up from your slumber. It is time to wake up and to stop playing church and religion. It is time to stop living for yourself and living with your lamps half-filled. It's time to learn how to live a life that's overflowing with the oil of the Holy Spirit.

You need to learn how to live a life just like Jesus Christ did. You need to know how to have the heart of Jesus and respond with the mind of Christ. I would encourage you all to start to read my books on Amazon one by one. They are only ninety-nine cents each, and I am sure that they won't put you to sleep if you read them and apply them to your life.

You can access my Amazon book page at
amazon.com/author/matthewrobertpayne.

I'd Love to Hear from You

One of the ways that you can bless me as a writer is by writing an honest and candid review of my book on Amazon. I always read the reviews of my books, and I would love to hear what you have to say about this one.

Before I buy a book, I read the reviews first. You can make an informed decision about a book when you have read enough honest reviews from readers. One way to help me sell this book and to give me positive feedback is by writing a review for me. It doesn't cost you a thing but helps me and the future readers of this book enormously.

To read my blog, request a life-coaching session, request your own personal prophecy, or receive a personal message from your angel, you can also visit my website at http://personal-prophecy-today.com. All of the funds raised through my ministry website will go toward the books that I write and self-publish.

To write to me about this book or to share any other thoughts, please feel free to contact me at my personal email address at survivors.sanctuary@gmail.com.

You can also friend request me on Facebook at Matthew Robert Payne. Please send me a message if we have no friends in common as a lot of scammers now send me friend requests. I am starting a community church meeting on Zoom and training people in the prophetic over the Zoom platform, so make sure you get in touch with me to be part of that.

You can also do me a huge favor and share this book on Facebook as a recommended book to read, which will help me and other readers.

How to Sponsor a Book Project

If you have been blessed by this book, you might consider sponsoring a book for me. It normally costs me $1,500—and sometimes more—to produce each book that I write, depending on the length of the book. If you seek the Holy Spirit about financing a book for me, I know that the Lord would be eternally grateful to you.

Consider how much this book has blessed you and then think of hundreds or even thousands of people who would be blessed by a book of mine. As you are probably aware, the vast majority of my e-books cost ninety-nine cents, which proves to you that book writing is indeed a ministry for me and not a money-making venture. I would be very happy if you supported me in this.

If you have any questions for me or if you want to know what projects I am currently working on that your money might finance, you can write to me at survivors.sanctuary@gmail.com and ask me for more information. I would be pleased to give you more details about my projects.

You can sow any amount into my ministry by simply sending me money via the PayPal link at this address: https://personal-prophecy-today.com/support-my-ministry/.

You can be sure that your support, no matter the amount, will be used for the publishing of helpful Christian books for people to read.

Suggested Further Reading

Intoxicated with Babylon by Steve Gallagher

Influencing Your World for Christ by Matthew Robert Payne

13 Tips to Becoming the Light of Christ by Matthew Robert Payne

Prophetic Evangelism Made Simple by Matthew Robert Payne

How to Hear God's Voice by Matthew Robert Payne

You can access my Amazon book page at amazon.com/author/matthewrobertpayne.

Acknowledgments

Jesus:

I want to thank you for being my lifelong friend and for never deserting me, no matter how dark my life became. You have led me into some great adventures. Being with you has filled my life with meaning.

Holy Spirit:

I want to thank you for leading and teaching me. You are a great teacher, better than I could ever be. You have been with me every step of the way. Thank you for your help with this book. You practically dictated it.

Father:

Thank you for loving me and entrusting me with this life that I am living. Thank you for revealing my purpose to me and leading me toward accomplishing it. Thank you so much for your Son, Jesus. Thank you for everything that you have done in my life. Thank you for leading me to help more people with another book. Thank you for your words in this book.

Art Miner:

Thank you so much for sharing your thoughts in this book. It's almost as if you read many of my previous books and put them into your own words. The confirmation was beautiful and much-needed and will greatly encourage the body of Christ.

Lisa Thompson:

I want to especially thank Lisa for editing this book of mine. You take my simple words and transform them to make me seem smarter than I really am.

If you have any editing needs, you can contact Lisa at writebylisa@gmail.com.

Alison Treat:

I want to thank Alison for being part of my team as a proofreader. I want to thank you for all the work that you did with this book to polish and improve it.

Friends:

I want to thank Darla, Lisa, Nicola, Mary, Laura, David Joseph, Michael Van Vlymen, David, Tufan, Andy, Ginny, and Ruth for your friendship and for how you have impacted my life.

Mom and Dad:

I want to thank my mother and father for all the love that they have given me. I am a product of your love.

Readers and ministry supporters:

I want to thank the readers of my books and my ministry supporters for the funds that you have given me to publish books. I live to educate people, and I thank my readers and the supporters of my ministry because you make life worth living.

About Matthew Robert Payne

Matthew Robert Payne, a teacher and prophet, enjoys writing what the Lord puts on his heart to share. He receives great pleasure from interacting with others on Facebook, hearing from people who have read his books, and prophesying over people's lives. He is a passionate lover of and disciple of Jesus Christ. He hopes that as you discover his books, you will intimately come to know Jesus, the Father, and Matthew through his transparent writing style.

Matthew grew up in a traditional Baptist church and gave his heart to Jesus Christ at the tender age of eight years old. But he left home at the age of eighteen, living a wild life for many years and engaging in bad habits and addictions. At twenty-seven, he was baptized in water and, at the same time, baptized in the Holy Spirit. Matthew learned about the five-fold ministry offices and received a revelation of their value today.

He started his journey as a prophet twenty years ago, learning about this gift and putting it into practice. With thousands of prophecies under his belt, he can confidently prophesy to friends and strangers alike. He has been writing for a number of years and self-published his first book in 2011. Today he spends his time earning money to self-publish and writes a new book approximately every month. You can find sixteen hundred of his videos on YouTube under Matthew Robert Payne.

You can connect with him on Facebook. You can sow into his book-writing ministry, read his blog, receive a message from your angel, or even receive your own nine-minute personal prophecy from Matthew at http://personal-prophecy-today.com.

BLURB

In *A Prophetic Word to the Church of America*, Art Miner addresses the American church with a sobering yet hopeful word. Matthew Robert Payne heard this word in a prophetic group and wanted to release it in this short book. Matthew then shares his perspective in a conversation with Art.

A seasoned prophet, Art addresses many issues in the body of Christ, including

- the problem of the sleeping church and how to solve it,
- the job of every believer,
- judging on outward appearance,
- increasing in intimacy with Jesus, and
- God's heart for the hurting and broken.

If you are looking for change in your life and if you want to take practical steps toward a deeper relationship with Christ, read this book today.

www.ingramcontent.com/pod-product-compliance
Lightning Source LLC
Chambersburg PA
CBHW031508040426
42444CB00007B/1257